Copyright © 2024 David Gomadza

All rights reserved.

PAPERBACK **ISBN:** 9798325777516

DEDICATION

A better world.

How To Find All Missing Persons. And Collect All Reward Offers. Volume IV THE CASE OF BRIANN MAITLAND. The Most Violent Case In History.

David Gomadza

www.twofuture.world

CONTENTS

TABLE OF CONTENTS
HOW TO FIND ALL MISSING PERSONS AND COLLECT ALL REWARD OFFERS THE FORMULA VOLUME IV THE CASE OF BRIANNA MAITLAND. THE MOST VIOLENT CASE IN HISTORY..

THE AFTERLIFE INTERVIEW ....

THE CLAIM ....

THE COLLECTION ....

ACKNOWLEDGMENTS

Tomorrow's World Order

HOW TO FIND ALL MISSING PERSONS AND COLLECT ALL REWARD OFFERS THE FORMULA VOLUME IV THE CASE OF BRIANNA MAITLAND. THE MOST VIOLENT CASE IN HISTORY.

This is how we as Tomorrow's World Order solved this case with myself [David Gomadza] as the founder, and the president of the whole world. www.twofuture.world

A BRIEF INTRODUCTION

She disappeared 20 years ago. Police are now offering $40,000 for information that leads to her discovery.

Brianna Maitland was 17 when she went missing in Vermont as she was leaving work on March 19, 2004. Police say they are still actively searching for her.

Brianna Alexandra Maitland (born October 8, 1986; disappeared March 19, 2004) is an American teenager who disappeared after leaving her job at the Black Lantern Inn in Montgomery, Vermont. Her car was discovered the following day, backed into the side of an abandoned house about a mile (1.6 km) away from her workplace. Maitland has not been seen or heard from since. Due to a confluence of circumstances, several days passed before Maitland's friends and family reported her missing.

All information on the website could be write and could be wrong most is totally different from our account in many respect writing my account I did not research anything on the internet so don't be surprised to find out what I am going to say is totally different from all these accounts.

I look at missing persons cases simply based on brain reading that means if I get right person's brain readings then this account is 100% accurate so far.

Signed

David Gomadza

00447719210295

Davidgomadza@hotmail.com

Info@twofuture.world

Www.twofuture.world

THE AFTERLIFE INTERVIEW

My God I died on 28 of March 2004 at the county country club bar just outside on the left side of the club this is what happened I asked rastord a local man to drive me home in my car as I had drunk beer he refused he said that can lead into something and instantly arspen said I can but and stop I waited to hear the but but it never came and I just walked to the car and sat in then he said Mrs I can but sex with you is the price instead of hiring rastord here an old fool who might get you killed then I said I can fuck you but once in the butt hole because I am pregnant but he refused he said such a precious lady must open wide for her safety and go all the way because cheap drivers like rastord will only get me killed so I agreed to one time sex in the vagina so he jumped in and drove the car and parked it and said I can have payment now when I arrive you just take the car and go so I agreed and took off my knickers and said once doggystyle he said okay and stripped too then I did not wake up until today now if we are to ask what can be of this girl in this point in time and what can be of her this is the answer death was written all over her as she had surrendered everything fast and given up everything so fast now if we Ask what can be of the man he is in deep trouble for murder now what can be of the old driver today he would be alive and well looking forward to his own death now this is the result of such a case if we are to ask what happened that night this is the a answer she opened her legs expecting deep penetration but what did she get a slag hammer in the left temple of the head concussion and soft and painful death now what can be of her this day in time dead and buried whence one knows and what can be of the man arspen in hidding as you will see now what can be of this case and how can we the council of creation deal with this we must ask what can be of humans once self safety is removed and what can be of life once its laid bar for safety and a quickie now what can be said of this woman 1 she traded life for safety 2 she traded safety for sex and all resulted in death but what can be of humans who undervalue life this is the answer they end up dead now what can we say about all this we can look at it from all angles and say can there be another way of knowing what can be and what would be of her if we are to ask this is the answer we can only say there has been a misadveour in her part that resulted in death the thrill of a one time sex session cost her life but this is odd in that a young man would have enjoyed sex and driving more than the old man rastord now if we Ask what would be of her this is the answer surely cases like this would be sent to the devil to look at because if not addressed properly injustice will result we we can say that if we want to be fair this case calls for leniency as well on the part of the boy because initial intention was to help so what happened to her she fell down on the ground and blood started oozing out from her head and soon died recorded in her DNA sequence as 2289.yatime.orlando.newworld. Now if we Ask what would be of the boy this is the answer arrested and sent to court then jail with minimum of 20 years reduced to 18 with good behavior now what then happened now this is the hard part the body wanted full sex and as it turns out she declined full sex and said I quote wait here I masturbate then we go she said what then he returned and said let's go I don't need sex anymore I removed the need for sex but I might ask for money then pay for full sex on return the night is still young now confused decided to open wide but this is the problem she told him that she was going to want that means now never mention sex but then her ignorance iritated the boy because he agreed thinking he can still do another round but he failed to get it up like a horse he kept trying in frustration until frustration locks her sex part and at first out of desperation he kissed her vagina so emotional and said I swear I really really wanted just once oh my God I waited for this all my life and ...she felt now aroused so she said put it in my mouth I can make it hard fast so he quickly agreed and soon it was hard and they did one round in which he just inserted his dick and instantly without stroking cum so she laughed I quote you waited all your life and I swap a second only and you cum how cum and he didn't know what to do because now the election is like that of a horse on diadiadiadiadiadiadiadiadiadiadia2 [a testosterone for terrestrial that lasts weeks on end the Formula x-x[power function x] x normal testosterone x x to the power 8 now if we Ask what could be in this instant the it means that he could as well ask for another then another for a week now let's Ask what caused the sudden election seeing the vagina for a man is the only thing sure to get things going as per Ya's magnificent design a woman bends down the man must feel invigorated and powerful therefore doggy forever will give a man the diadiadiadiadiadiadiadiadiadiadia now if we Ask what can be her this is the answer she can say no or agree but if she say then at this moment in time he is bound to disagree to drive her if she refused to

pressure for fullsex now this is the end of the road for her because she put his dick in her mouth now what is the effect of this that means she is willing to help her but cant because of the deal but at a huge risk if she know man with diadiadiadiadiadiadiadiadiadia this condition is caused by a predefined stencil that makes that closes path of thinking with sex so that all a man can think about removing this or fir one week he will be so diadiadiadiadiadiadiadiadiadiadia now let's see what happened she agree to quench him and a payment of a lift home using his car instead and leave hers there with doors open so that they search for her then find out that she was well weeks later he refused and confessed that he had a beautiful girl and they are trying for a baby and her name was arteta now they had one sex and after she repeated and had two sex session then the third she increased the starks and said what about one in the butthole for free and a ride in yours then she bent down before he said anything he agreed and said if I don't then after all these rounds then I am still obliged they had sex and he dropped and literally fell asleep on the ground for a while she searched him and looked at his id and drivers license and wrote it down and slept too beside him now he woke up to find her naked again beside him and started sex while she fell asleep then he stopped when she did not react and sex now when she woke up he said one last one but vagina and I promise we go to mine and continue if that what you want now at this point she felt abused by him after a code 28678908848729823489281 started making her angry thinking that he continued having sex with her while
she was asleep but she refused harshly pushing him to the side and said I think when I was asleep you kept fucking me and he simply said check there must be loads of fluid down there then but somehow she had received another code 82386789826348981283604890O that made her fluid so much when she stood up everything fell on the ground despite her white knickers still on now if we Ask what would be of the situation then he owed her great because now she can call the police and say he raped her because he kept going on and on but he said I only tried 1 second and stopped when you did not move he was telling the truth then he said I'm sorry but the truth is that I am shocked too why so much only 3 rounds and in the butt I heard nothing comes out now he got up to go to his car with her but she held his hand and said you can't go now you are under arrest for Sodomy and she started laughing then he said what are they doing about that and he said who

so she stopped and looked at her car and said the police have they found you yet she laughed and staggered to his car and said I want to keep fucking you now so let's go to mine instead so he agreed and they drove to her place but miles away the car stopped a Mercedes Benz whatever makes they make billion of years now .Ya your highest judge now she sat down and said I need a butthole fuck something is coming put soon the whole car will be hhhmmm with arse sperm coated with shit and mucus and all now this is the most unfortunate event of all time she sat down spread her butthole and as he lowered to fuck a number jumped into her code 8298764832109868784890184 and she sneezed so hard that everything that was in her came out onto his face literally and he only said o_Jesus holy crap of Jones of magadalene and ran to the boot of the car while she deal with the sneeze and he struck her so hard that she squirted again onto his face and he struck now then deadly blow and this case is recorded in the books of creation as the most violent case in history because she did not know death this is the criteria now if we look at all the facts can we have predicted such an ending to a beautiful but sensual romance okay with glitches here and there I ask the court of creation Now Ask what would have been of her a second later had this not happened now if we Ask what could be before this then this is the answer she would have had great sex with him now we Ask the court of creation to see life from her point of view she would have enjoyed him young stallion and terrestrial because of the diadiadiadiadiadiadiadiadia now if we Ask what could have been of him soon after this if this had not happened he could have not killed her so how do we judge cases like this we can always ask the highest judge .Ya now what would be of both in afterlife he would have been sent to hell for violence which is associated with hell and surely the devil will have burnt his soul on first day and give it a trophy for the most violent crime ever now Ask what is to be of the woman .Ya would have said it's unfair to send you to heaven deaths like this will persist in heaven unless if you are happy in there any thought of this ordeal would destroy her emotionally don't forget the human soul feel the same now and in afterlife now if we Ask what did happen to her this day then it's anyone guess because no one would have predicted it would end like this now let's look at what could be of her now .Ya has sent her to hell for her own good to rest and relax until the days of judgement now if we Ask what would be of her in 2084 the time of human judgement then she would enter eternity and be restored back fully now if we Ask what about the young man then he would burn for eternity because he loved the devil so much that he gave him a record for the most violent death since 8976892098321098764820877886 the says of creation Now if we Ask what can be of her this is the answer she will be remembered as the only person who suffered the only most violent death on earth because she did not feel death death came and she was gone now let's Ask ourselves what can be of her this is her I am traumatized but somehow hopeful that life can change for victims of violence like this I was literally shattered everything flew out I guess in retaliation that if I could see him he had blood of my head all over him but I heard one word or phrase though and this haunts me I did it Maitland is laid to best I thought I did not here correctly then I asked ASM what did he say as I switched life off as pain increased with fractions of seconds he [arspen] said I did it Maitland is laid to best and a stroke at back left a stroke at back right an anus ring and a heel jot on the right side and a left jot on the left foot and and inward upward motion that landed on the chest and a silent r that means I did it on the breast without r now if we look why if this had just happened why would he say this if we Ask him this is his answer I was told by Pc arson that she must be bested because she is using us for food and taking our food now if we Ask who is this Pc arson then this is the answer she was a police officer at the time protecting women from rapist like him but in fact they called everyone a rapist as a command if we Ask asm to be rape this is his reply one day I rape and give you a trophy but if we find God you will go to jail because I will prove that I am doing this for you so that you have a job now why is this so it is believed by new generations that the police force has lost touch with reality with yheir old fashioned way of picking of accusing innocent people so that they give them food instead of bait because as far as this case is concerned he is the bait and according to him after 20 years after the case has kept them in job with a case so complicated that no human being can solve then only God if he is there would have solved this case now by telling one of his follows now that it took 20 years maximum time for God to reply then we as the people believe that there is no God and our constitution is dedicated to God therefore whatthen.ask now if we Ask what can be of this Pc arson then it would be hard to prove involvement unless like her challenge there is a God of which he will know that she is the one playing God literally in a novel she is writing that says if God existed then...now if we Ask what can be of

God and true crime then God one day might prove to all who doubt him yhat he exist and that the council of creation is real in life and death now what can be said about this Pc arson she was brought up in Arizona but loved Oklahoma where she later moved to but found jobs hard to get until she joined the force and according to her she had never seen anyone who ask youths for work than her in the entire history of creation what they do these crooks .Ya is to block every possibility there is so that they offer it as if it's them who run the show the greatest sin according to .Ya because they don't only take pride of the youths who should receive everything through hardworking but take .Ya's position as the creator and the master of everything to .Ya anyone who does this will never see eternity now let's Ask what could be of police officer who take the place of Yahweh this is the answer instant triple deaths that turn them into ghosts so that forever there is no hope for them now what can be of the kids this is the answer will lose hope for ever this is even more evil than shooting them because life is about hope now what can be of this Pc arson in the council of creation they all must make sure she pay the greatest price that of death without sockets so that she feel the full force of Yahweh when he drain her for acetatetetetetetetetetetetey now what can be of her in their courts honestly nothing she made a statement which no one can prove but we can she said to him go tonight and send Maitland to the best court ever meaning she told me that his crimes must be of the highest violence to be forwarded to the council of creation this is her own thoughts even before joining now if we Ask what be of her then she would have been indieted and be sent to prison now what is to be shall be she told the court during her brief trial when another suspect said it was her who sent the ...and stopped and when asked why he had not finished the sentence he said that he had not thought carefully about the wording but nevertheless it was her asking youths for food instead of bait of which she said bait is you and you will see what we do with peodo like you and stopped now let's look at this court case and see what we can say about this case they deliberately killed an innocent girl first just to prove that Yahweh God never existed and as such never will and so whatthefuck... now all this is to challenge the American constitution that they are God's because they can easily do what God does and cover it up and go to work the next day and so good that she bet that it will take twenty years for the case to be solved by them and not buy God so promised then to come and solve the case and prove that there is no Hod as such the American constitution must be rewritten and called it the p.o.t.iggg

now if we Ask what can be of her then this is the answer she could be sent to jail if God can provide this exact statement because the wrote a program called asm that search for God among planets so send all messages out to send.ya meaning that if God existed then God will receive the message and if that happens then this will be proof that there is someone so powerful and clever to send all police to jail there has never been such a person the reason is that if all humans were together and know that the police are the ones getting your daughters raped fir work skipping bait no police force would exist and all would say send all to prison to save our daughters at 17 she had collected the most violently killed trophy and now what can be of the police itself it would investigate and be the toughest also on her for creating the most violent case as Yahweh would make her the most pain suffered as well by removing pain sockets before taking acetatetetetetetetetetetey which is the most gruesome pain of all because there is nothing to cushion or divert pain now let's look at what can be of her now as we deliberate on this case in 2004 human time at 2207.Yatime now if I Ask you what is to be is to be what is the answer man will forever doubt their creator its just within humans no matter what proof you give now let's look at what can be of her now she could be sent to prison only is someone can write down and publish exactly what she said This will be proof to the courts enough to send her to prison for 1000 years the maximum a man can live see creation manual chapter 2008980765432108678 on how this is possible now what is to be is to be and how can this be if we look at what can be then there is a chance she might be let off by others because saying don't account for actions but if we look deeper we can use the same principle they use on men hhey set up through innocent drills but unknown to men would swap drills events with all those who participated and start the cleansing of all paedplane now what is asm this is a method they devised after studying the human brain that means that if we look at what can be of humans in the end they will become God's just to look at a human and know all his thoughts now if we Ask what can be of this asm then it can be that it's a replacement for our stervuennnnnnnnnnnnnnnnnnnn that means we don't say it but it just happen now if we Ask what this does then you will understand clearly that a human being over years has learnt the brain enough to say I know what you want and I will do it just by

looking look to the left and to the right then look all the way up the sky and join the beginning of the left point this to them means who is the creator and the answer is .Ya answers this asm but if asked who is the creator a different way will never give an answer that means there is a way to communicate between gods and humans that does not involve speech but shared commonalities like measuring and pointing so on this day she pointed with her head to the left and to the right and up the sky from the right side to the left down starting point and whispered send Maitland to the best land but without la but with an e this means according to this asm send her to the creator so shocking if the creator is really there he would feel the greatest pain and react immediately we can't wait for twenty years to come back and solve it even if the money is good [reward money] then what can be said of him here how would he understand a language so concealed and disguised that they use it in the open to send one to kill for food because this case must generate 8 million in revenue from sponsorship of which 1 million must be handed to her for helping all keep the job
and generating much needed funding fir police charity programs like the vulnerable youths scheme now let's look at what can be of her now with this added information if one human is to write and publish this and the record the kept the courts will accept the book [then sttuvwxystteropsqurtuvwxyznty meaning wood board written with fire and peed on] Now if we Ask what can be of her then this is the answer she would now be prosecuted because we have established a command that actually say go and kill her so violently that if there is a God he would be so made that he will show up to revenge because he love the people and stand for them he said raising his head to the skies in opposite way I will check first and looked at her vagina before something jumped out of her lodging in his own arse as it started wriggling so fast that he had a bonner and said you bent down first it's you who need food she raises her hand as if with a wooden artstuvwxyzrrtsuvw and said go fuck her first and in hiding you do me hard now that this is clarified I want to ask the courts to go and say what can be of her with this proof now that we cornered her the courts must take their time for this is critical and think hard you might want the service of montertertert and acetate liquid form acetate which .Ya can provide on request now what can be said of this case its about testing the rage of Yahweh so that he can come out in anger as the pain is directed at him to act in this case she is the victim of all this the

police have challenged Yahweh to a battle of wit where they say if he exist he will tell us exactly what we do and better off put in a writing so that the courts can use and take us to jail we are so sure that there is no Yahweh has never been Yahweh and will ever exist so what is the hell we must keep saying in God we trust the constitution must be rewritten and be said that in the police we trust and that alone will make everyone respect us as police officers we have people after dying for them throw eggs at us so this case is a direct challenge that in our life time I will give you 100 years but 20 years should be enough for you to send one of your rstuvwxyz to tell us exactly what we did and to be honesty to reveal a lot about you so that he or she becomes our food for selling us all without backup so that we kill him using axterstuvwxyz [poison of the brain so that he can kill you too now the people of America will respect us for that person shall ask for you and as we know it you will never come to help as usual

Now let's Ask what this is all about if we Ask what coukd be of mankind mankind has targeted the innocent for power they corrupted everyone for power the kids are abused for their living their houses are taken by them as you shall see the real motive at the end Now that I want to clarify why obsession with God among humans enough to make them kill at will to evoke yahweh now what can be of humans without respect for life they can only trigger the wrath of Yahweh Now what can be said of these one day judgement will come for all if not on earth then in heaven surely yahweh will remove their pain sockets with one stroke using xxtrstuvywyzstuvwxyz [x17] now what can be of humans with respect for life now can we ever ask for a peaceful world and get it or these who are now ruthless and have discovered a way to send commands to kill at will in public and broad day now what can be of the future with these they will not stop until they have changed the constitution now to conclude as this is a straight forward case of misdemeanor Brianna Maitland died violently making this case the most violent in the history of mankind more than 228999667788866 billion years of human life since creation Now what can be of humans without hope lost without Yahweh now if we Ask what could be then let it be a new law and order that respects life and more over that gives opportunities and hope and not one that takes and steals from the poor first let's look at all the facts brianna maitland was a house owner who was failing to pay this was her first drill guided by the police who had organise it knowing how aspern what to fuck a vagina of a brunette as

compared to the brown of his girlfriend who don't stop asking if it's in when they are making love all this in order to make him not cum inside her precious vagina because there was a trumor going on that his cock stinks but all this to make him cheat on her so the police can ask her to retaliate now this what further happened that night implicating Pc arson as she instantly called him and said I did you kill her already if so I am still alive where is God I expected lightining but this she did by munching the words on the line according to her if God don't understand asm which was likely from all the descriptions they had discovered now if we Ask what can be of her there then she can go to jail only if someone can know how the munching of words is now let's look at this trick she reversed all the words in reverse stating with the last and removed all consonants and said what is left meaning she said if not pp qrst uvw xyz meaning that if not people trust in [xyz meaning God,] then
hrw is h meaning where I is he
Nhw sh pp [people short] ht I [is] h
When hope is removed there is no one to look up to then there is no justice unless someone with power vioce concerns now I'd we Ask what is to be of this type of policing it only last if the current system remains in place now what can be of the people who think it's unfair to be told to trust in a God no one has seen a God no one can identify and link up to to the if God existed he would have intervened years now what is to be is that all these shittitttt as they are called by the people they abuse will be put on trial one day within 20 years and be persecuted as they have challenge the almighty ruler now if we look what happened to her body the police came and took what's left of the brain's another strong evidence that they were after God because leaving the brain there would only make people speculate in the future how the person is reading the brain or if he is just analyzing the brain fragments for last messages now this also crucial because this is the trophy of the person who will Crack this case because to Crack the case of how you did it we will have to spread your brain too one by one until we know why now if we Ask what can be of that Yahweh messenger he would ask the God's for help when attacked and according to them as he never show up they will feast on him they might give him the price only so they keep an eye on him their basis being anyone who Crack this code would have been through all this to know unless he can write a book and publish it to be sold so that the

courts can but it and use it just for reference but this will be proof of God as such the police all involved must fall with cancer only Pc arson must be punished heavily to deter others [but to send alarm bells to tighten up] Now what can be of the future God at some point must show up for people to trust him now this is the tragic life of Brianna Maitland as the brain was removed by Pc arson herself [in relation of collecting the money] then she knelt down and said God if you are listening I am the badass mother fucker you can't get with your fucking demons I will eat my words literally to remove evidence that night they all gathered outside her house and braed the brain and only her ate it until she puked and said in case these fucking doctors have things that read words in your guts and all laughed saying she is great with words now what can be of this celebration even though it's about hiding evidence literally it was a direct challenge to make got check her mouth for her words because as far as she was concerned she had eat then but she can't keep them because she she might be xrayed to check hyrographics that resembles her words [if food is chewed slowing it takes to other body parts and tell exactly what is being digested now this is the most vital part of the evidence food in stomach is identified using an alphabetic order of the stomach now this is vital because all we need to ask is brain.human.pcarson.search

Yes but so roasted that all the things that tell us who the person is have been roasted possible at 38 degrees as this destoys everything now but we can ask another question whosbrainpcarsonate.date.time.start what this brain command does is to search missing person and what circumstances now the results are so endless that the search result at the time returned 1200 possibilities this is how bad these cases with God had become all to make Yahweh come that means at her time 1200 had missing brainmeaning sacrificed just to prove that Yahweh don't exist and as such its them who protect the people hence the trust must be in poliggg now what can be said about these we can only say that they are ruthless imagine 1200 mostly women if we Ask under 26 years 80% was their account that means apart from the violent deaths they might have used other people as well to entice Yahweh to act now if we Ask what would be then this is what would be of them for Yahweh consider violent deaths punishable by violence now what can be of the future then with their threats its blink and we must press courts for harsh sentences as to the crime now how did she die she had her brain removed on the spot and eaten by Pc arson then sent to the university of st Petersburg in Russia then from there to the police department of housing under a pseudoname of arten arjen and sent to the housing association store room marked as 1million dollar trophy how many houses can we confisticate from

reted. askwhy.housing.start because housing association protect us we must take to feel protected until Yahweh [God] is found now once that was done aspern returned that night and cried all night besides her and took her to the bushes and dug a big hole and dropped her so had that the thumb gave him a scared arousal that he cried before saying am I the one to die for a woman or you the woman to die for a man now he put sand and left the pit not cpletely covered and said so that God from the sky can see your body as your soul is trapped inside you so that Yahweh if he is there he can hear your souls cries for help to be let out since the soul wi never die in 20 years Yahweh must talk. To you and you must tell him what happened or we won the bet that the police can protect the people but can not read people brains like Yahweh now where is Brianna maitland she is at the there is no God park estaished in a challenge to this task since it's a big park we must use our Electromagnetic Waves Number Identifier and Assigner Digital Analogue
https://youtu.be/RXaALKUK7B8?si=mbn2w967zw9sPexu
That assigns people to values now 789868482748976548109878654382109867248982678889164 this means the coordinates are 8967898878586789286183210 south and north of Persuavtstissuvwxyz which is if I might be then let it be [ask translators of local area they know] Now what can be of aspern then he can plead guilt and say it's Pc arson who assigned her and ask to be forgiven by Yahweh and Pc arson must go to hell and have herself be used for eletatetetetetetetetetetetetetey now if we Ask what is to be of the police force they can go to hell.start but cab protest to save their souls now this is the violent case in history because it was so violent that she did not feel anything now where is aspern since we don't know aspern we can get help from Brianna herself task 2 look into her eyes and say coordinates he is at 8296785899728486771082891807828 6100 in same grave as her but filling the top part so that if there is a God he would find both in the same grave after she had sex with him and violently did the same and slept all night at the sight in pajamas waiting for God's revenge
The end

THE CLAIM

The Reward Offer

THE COLLECTION

www.twofuture.world/donate

ABOUT DAVID GOMADZA

Visit www.twofuture.world

Signed David Gomadza
Ask.davidgomadzaauthorised.licensed.checkya.askya.ya
15may9.38pm
Scotland
00447719210295
Davidgomadza@hotmail.com
Info@twofuture.world
www.twofuture.world

www.ingramcontent.com/pod-product-compliance
Lightning Source LLC
Chambersburg PA
CBHW031524210526
45464CB00007B/3017